A First-Start Easy Reader

This easy reader contains only 56 different words, repeated often to help the young reader develop word recognition and interest in reading.

Basic word list for *What a Dog!*

to
go
a
he
for
I
am
too
and
not
on
out
the
run
is
his
can
dog
woof

barks
wants
walk
will
take
very
busy
says
goes
lawn
they
over
into
woods
next
time
wait
who

whom
Bernie
Bernie's
mother
father
sister
brother
Sue
Bob
Billy
little
splash
puddle
ouch
bush
walking
until
leash
what

What a Dog!

Written by Sharon Gordon

Illustrated by Deborah Sims

Troll Associates

Printed in the United States of America.

ISBN 0-89375-293-2

10 9 8 7 6 5 4 3 2

“Woof! Woof!” barks Bernie.

Bernie wants to go for a walk.

What a dog!

can walk Bernie.

and his brother...

and his sister...

Next time, little Billy will wait until

his mother and his father…

Who is walking whom?

Ouch! Into a bush they run.

Splash! Into a puddle they run.

Into the woods they run.

Over the lawn they run.

Out go Bernie and Billy.

On goes Bernie's leash.

"I will take Bernie for a walk."

"I am not busy,"

says little Billy.

"Woof! Woof!" barks Bernie.

"And, I am too busy,"

says brother Bob.

"I am too busy,"

says sister Sue.

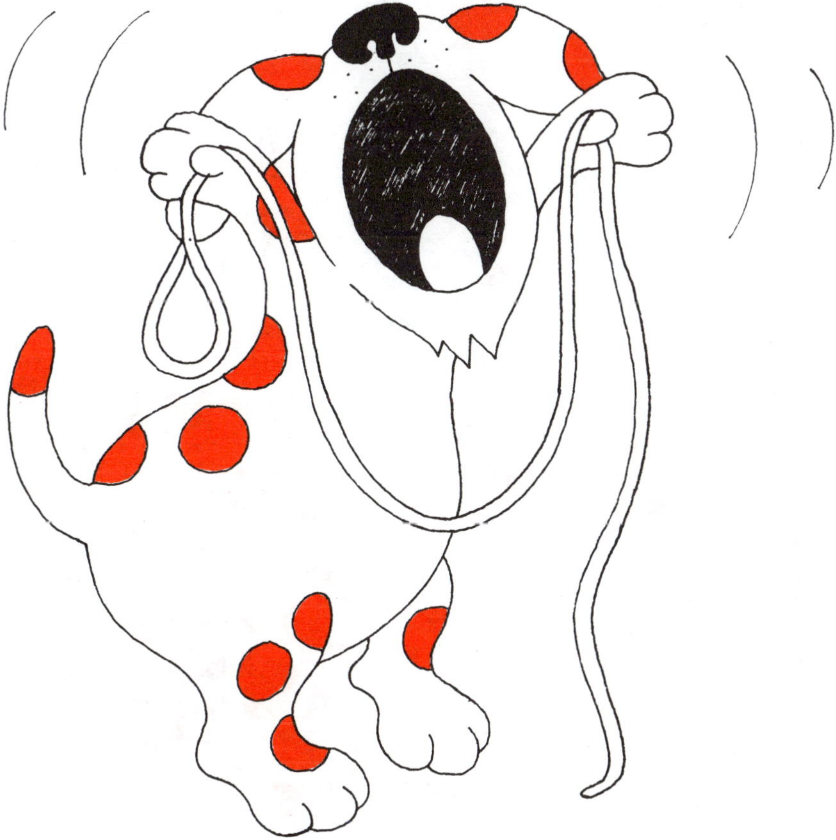

“Woof! Woof!” barks Bernie.

“I am very busy,” says Mother.

“Woof! Woof!” barks Bernie.

"I am very busy," says Father.

Who will take Bernie for a walk?

"Woof! Woof!" he barks.